THE SPIRITUAL HERO'S JOURNEY
WORKBOOK

Imprint

The Spiritual Hero's Journey
Copyright © 2020 Julia Charakter
Translated from the German by Gitta Wolf

Herstellung und Verlag: BoD - Books on Demand, Norderstedt

ISBN: 9783752627497

info@juliacharakter.de

YOGA-DIARY.DE

The Spiritual
Hero's Journey
Workbook

"If you do follow your bliss you put yourself on a kind of track that has been there all the while, waiting for you, and the life that you ought to be living is the one you are living. Follow your bliss and don't be afraid, and doors will open where you didn't know they were going to be."

— Joseph Campbell

GOING HOME

The spiritual path is walked by many, though there are many directions. And everyone is on their own path. It all starts with the call. For the meaning of life, for lasting bliss, for growth or for peace. And then the journey begins. A journey that takes place on the inside as well as on the outside. On our way to our true self we encounter mentors, allies, shadows and negative experiences, we lose old relationships and in return find new ones. We meet our own shadows, our fears, and threshold guardians who make us doubt whether we are even heading in the right direction. Then we come across old blockages, monsters, and other stumbling blocks. Our inner purification processes can sometimes be very painful. We fall down and we take our time until we are strong again. We get up and continue to walk. Everyone on the spiritual path is aware of these stages, which are very similar to the stages of the Hero's Journey. And although every story is different, most stories have a similar structure – that's what the Hero's Journey is about. It is based on the theory of archetypes in the collective unconscious by C.G. Jung as well as Joseph Campbell who, on the basis of this as well as thousands of legends, myths and stories, devised a story meta-structure. In a way, every spiritual development resembles the Hero's Journey. All of us on the spiritual path encounter similar challenges and the same questions, and that's what this book is about. This book is for all those who are fellow travellers on this path – into the profound depths of their life, their consciousness and their soul. It is a Spiritual Hero's Journey, which in the end will take us all back home.

How the Hero's Journey Came into my Life

In my professional life as an author and film maker I have worked extensively with the Hero's Journey model. It is a universal formula for all stories, myths, and fairy tales that carry within them a deep truth. It is also applicable to the personal stories we experience in our own life. The source – or the foundation that the Hero's Journey is built on – is the archetypes set out by Carl Gustav Jung, a student of Freud, who explored the unconscious. He discovered the existence of a universal unconscious and found that every culture has its symbols, specific characters and personality types. To name but a few: Hero, Mentor, Shadow, Villain.

Joseph Campbell devoted his entire life to this theory. He gathered stories from all over the world, compared them, and discovered astonishing parallels. The purpose of all stories is to impart a collective higher truth, so that the listeners, readers, or viewers learn from the hero's experiences something of relevance to their own life as well as universal humanness, morality and ethics.

My Own Hero's Journey

My Ordinary World used to be the stressful editorial office of a TV company. Working for television, I was so overworked on a daily basis that eventually I had a terrible accident. Suddenly unable to move, I was forced to focus inwards upon what is important in life. It was the beginning of my first deliberate Hero's Journey, and I purposefully embarked on the pursuit of happiness. My personal Hero's Journey then became a physical journey and I travelled the world, visiting 12 countries and, ultimately, the deep layers of my soul: I had not, as initially expected, left all my shortcomings, gnawing inadequacies and unresolved problems behind – I had taken them all along on my trip around the world. At first, I tried to run away from this serious conflict, tried to forget and just have a good time. But in the end, there was no other way than to face all my shadows, face all my fears. It took five months before I finally found what I'd been looking for. I had found my Elixir, my own personal Holy Grail: spiritual practice. A regular yoga and meditation practice, an encounter with my guru, Amma, and all the experiences I'd had in India enabled me to return to the world I'd been accustomed to. But I was no longer the person I'd been before. The newly acquired spirituality was like an elixir that enriches my life to this day and provides positive, enjoyable guidance and direction. I discovered within me what I had spent all my life searching for outside of me. And now I faced another Hero's Journey.

Chapter 1

THE ORDINARY WORLD

STAGE 1

The Ordinary World is the beginning as well as the end of an archetypal hero-story, which means that the Hero's Journey model resembles a cycle. However, this segment is concerned solely with the beginning of the story.

> "Most stories take the hero out of the ordinary,
> mundane world and into a Special World, new
> and alien." (Vogler, The Writer's Journey. 10)

The Beginning: Our Home

The Hero's Journey begins at home, or in an environment that seems safe and familiar to us. It is, in a way, our comfort zone. The place we call home, where we can simply be who we are.

The Buddha's Golden Palace

The Buddha, for example, was the son of a king and lived in a huge palace with extensive gardens. He had the most delicious foods, expensive clothes, beautiful women who served him and hoped to marry him. Living within such a protected environment, he had very little comprehension of anything that existed outside of this Ordinary World. But boredom and discontent had crept into his everyday life. There was something within him that pushed him towards change. Although Asita the Wise had predicted his fate, his father swore to do everything within his power to ensure he would succeed him to the throne. But even though the king kept spoiling his son with many women and worldly pleasures,

Siddhartha grew more and more bored. He no longer desired any of these worldly things. He became increasingly curious about the world that was waiting for him outside the palace gates.

Something is Rotten in the Ordinary World

The beginning of the story takes us into the hero's Ordinary World. We meet the hero in his[1] often very safe and comfortable, but also somewhat boring, everyday life. However nice it all is, the hero knows that he has exhausted all means of further development. He is well protected but at the same time tied down and not free, in some subtle way even imprisoned. This, then, is fertile ground for the Call to Adventure. The safe Ordinary World forms a great contrast to the new, exciting, adventurous world that the hero is about to enter.

Your Own Hero's Journey
Homework No. 1 - Dare!

Every one of us is on his or her own Hero's Journey. This is why the Hero's Journey template can help us to understand where we are in our journey. This homework asks us to explore our own comfort zone.

Think: what makes you feel safe? What is your personal comfort zone? Make a list with 3 columns:

1. This is where I feel safe and comfortable
2. This makes me feel unsafe
3. This requires courage but I would love to do it!

---

[1] To avoid the clunky 'he or she' and 'his or hers' when referring to the hero (who might of course be a heroine), 'he' and 'his' are used throughout as generic pronouns.

Comfort zone	Feels uncomfortable	Requires courage

This comparison is a great method to figure out where you stand, what your safe, Ordinary World is, and what personal challenges you have in your life that you try to avoid – or where you don't yet have the aspiration or the courage to take the next step. It is also useful to know what you regard as the opposite of safe, namely the list of what makes you feel "unsafe". Just looking at these things will make you a little less afraid of them. It's always good to name your fear, it defuses it straight away. And the third column shows you what you desire, what your heart secretly calls for.

Chapter 2

THE CALL TO ADVENTURE

The second stage of the Hero's Journey begins with a Call. This may be a strong longing from within the hero's self, or a Call to Adventure from the outside world; some kind of "invitation to adventure", an opportunity that suddenly presents itself and causes the hero to turn towards a new direction.

Sometimes the need to take action may come because the status quo – the Ordinary World – is, like everything in life, subject to change. The Call can also present a problem. The hero finds himself confronted with a great change. The Ordinary World has altered, and the hero is faced with a challenge. For example, he may have to rescue someone, solve a case, embark on a great journey, fight for love, find a treasure, right a wrong, make a dream come true, change the direction of his life.

The Call seems to cast doubt on the ordinary, safe life. The hero is faced with a decision: will he dare to step into the unknown?

Call to Action

If the hero accepts the Call, it will in time become a Call to Action. The Ordinary World cannot continue to exist as it used to. Something must change. So this is a "Call to Action", an invitation to act.

Spiritual Heroes Long for Depth and Meaning

Prince Siddhartha, the Future Buddha, longed to experience the world outside of his palace gates. Disguised and accompanied by his charioteer, he left the palace compound and went to observe the people in a nearby park. During the first evening's outing, Siddhartha saw a *"decrepit old man, broken-toothed, gray-haired, crooked and bent of body"* (J. Campbell, The Hero with a Thousand Faces, p. 56). Having never before seen such an old person, he was profoundly moved, because he now understood that growing old is the fate of all life. During his next outing he saw a diseased man and was again deeply moved by his fate. On his next walk he saw, for the first time in his life, a dead man, and this encounter left the deepest impression on him. And during his final evening walk the Future Buddha encountered a monk. Siddhartha, amazed by his dignified appearance and his meticulous, agreeable clothing, again asked the charioteer who this person was.

"Sire, this is one who has retired from the world (…) The thought of retiring from the world was a pleasing one to the Future Buddha." (Campbell, pp. 57-58)

The Call can be a defining moment on the Spiritual Hero's Journey. I may experience and comprehend something at a deep level, such as a sacred book that allows me to see the world in a different light. An encounter with a guru, a saint or a monk might also be an experience that initiates the hero's Inner Call. Such unforgettable experiences and encounters cause us to rethink the Ordinary World and to question our ordinary life, which leads us to the need for a new direction.

After the Call, the story really gets under way. The hero is no longer undecided, staying put and stagnating in the comfort of the Ordinary World is no longer an option. The hero feels this Inner Call, this calling for action, for change. He has no option but to leave, to change or to act, even though this will encompass danger as well as a potential for growth.

"This first stage of the mythological journey – which we have designated the "call to adventure" – signifies that destiny has summoned the hero and transferred his spiritual center of gravity from within the pale of his society to a zone unknown. This fateful region of both treasure and danger may be variously represented: as a distant land, a forest, a kingdom underground, beneath the waves, or above the sky, a secret island, a lofty mountaintop, or profound dream state." (Campbell, p. 58)

Your Own Hero's Journey
Homework No. 2

When you are first faced with the Call, the natural reflex is the "Refusal" (Stage 3 of the Hero's Journey). That's why it's important to be aware of the Call. It requires a connection to your inner self, to the intuitive inner voice we all have within us. Awareness of our intuition and following our inner ca ling are part and parcel of every spiritual and inner Hero's Journey. We often ignore the Call because the entire order of everything, our entire Ordinary World, is at stake. People are frightened of change.

Your Inner Voice – Training Your Intuition

Find a quiet place where no one will disturb you, sit in whatever (meditation-) posture is comfortable, close your eyes and calm your breathing. Allow yourself to go deeply within. Ask yourself:

What is my calling?

What are my talents and how can I use them to serve?

What is calling me in my life right now?

What adventure awaits me?

Listen to your inner Self and wait for an intuitive answer. Take a pen and write them down. Be open to whatever your inner voice replies. If no reply comes, it is safe to assume that right now is not the time – or maybe you are already well under way!

Chapter 3

THE REFUSAL

STAGE 3.

The Call has reached the hero, but the hero isn't yet one hundred percent prepared to follow through. He is hesitant, not sure whether he would really be able to walk this path. This is an agonizing phase, one of swaying back and forth, of pondering options. But this phase is an essential part of each Hero's Journey – it is called "Hesitation" or "Refusal". Everything new carries risks. But: *"A magic dwells in each beginning"* (H. Hesse, Steps). Adventure awaits. However, there is this fear of the new, fear of freedom, fear of total independence.

Fear of the Future?

Above all, this is about fear of the unknown. Fear of the future. A refusal of the changes continually offered by life. We all know this. The future and the unknown can seem very threatening indeed. A door opens and you know it would be good to take this opportunity, but then fear of change comes up and you'd rather just stay home. Or you hesitate before you actually take a new direction. This is the stage where you might "overthink". You've not taken one step, the adventure hasn't even started yet, but you're already considering turning back.

Or you might lose yourself in *"... other interests. (...)*
Walled in boredom, hard work, or 'culture', the subject
loses the power of significant affirmative action."

(Campbell, p. 59)

How many projects have bitten the dust at this stage? How many relationships have never made it past this point, before they had even really started? How many spiritual paths have stopped right here because you didn't dare to take the next step? That's why it's so important to get past this stage of Refusal and just carry on walking.

Can I Do It?

The ability to follow the Call to Adventure mostly requires one thing: courage. Courage that a hero may not yet possess. Maybe there are feelings of inferiority, old blockages or fears that need dealing with before the journey can truly begin. It requires patience and the willingness to get out of "living in your mind". Because worries are like rocking chairs – they keep you rocking in place and get you nowhere.

The Buddha's Path to Freedom

The Buddha's walks outside the palace walls, where he had encountered an old man, a diseased man, a dead man and a saintly monk, awakened in him the call for a deeper meaning of life. He instinctively felt that for him, the right path was to renounce the world and live the life of a saint, but he also knew he had a long way to go. And even though he had received the four signs that had initiated within him the Call, on the other side there was still his Ordinary Life. He was married, had just become a father, and in his kingdom, he was the only heir to the throne. His father would do anything to keep him there and of course, Siddhartha himself had doubts whether he would even be able to overcome all those obstacles. Back then, a father's word was law. Every child had to obey and do whatever the head of the family decreed. This then was the conflict facing the Future Buddha: on the one hand he was drawn to following the Spiritual Call, knew this to be his path and his purpose. On the other hand, he had obligations to his family and his worldly commitments, and he was obliged to obey his father. Hesitation was a necessary intermediary stage.

Not to Follow the Call?

Often, walking your own spiritual path involves turning away from old friends or your family in order to embark on your personal, individual journey. This is not at all easy. The Ordinary World is just so comfortable, so safe, and this stage of avoidance often results in the Refusal of the Call. That's why many intentions and vocations fall by the wayside at this point. When that happens, there is no development, no new experiences, and the hero (often dissatisfied with himself) remains stuck in his Ordinary World.

Your Own Hero's Journey
Homework No. 3

We often hesitate when change beckons. Whenever we are facing an important decision, the request – the Call to Adventure – is met with fear of the unknown and a tendency to retreat. Sometimes we retreat many times. But in the end, the hero takes his courage in both hands and sets out on his adventure, filled with hope and confidence.

Courage is something we can learn. Homework No. 1 asked you to make a 3-column list, the one in the middle being the things you fear, your "courage list". From that list, take two or three items and do them. This won't be easy. Maybe it's ringing a friend you haven't spoken to in a long time. Or travelling alone to a place that will make your soul rejoice. Whatever the items on your "courage list", tackle them! One by one. And watch how your life changes for the better as a result.

1)

2)

3)

Chapter 1

MEETING THE GURU

STAGE 4

In Stage 3 – Refusal – the hero draws back into himself. The Call, this new state of affairs, seems a risky undertaking where his comfort zone and safety are at stake. So the hero refuses to accept the invitation to adventure. Maybe he has not yet developed the mindset to imagine being able to achieve his new goal. Or maybe it's the fear of the unknown, because choosing a new direction always requires courage. How can this phase of doubts and hesitation be overcome?

The Hero Needs Encouragement!

Wishing to conquer the Refusal stage, the hero will need support. It's practically impossible to do this on one's own, without any help. Also, sometimes it may be a good idea not to dive head-first into an adventure! It can be most helpful to prepare for a journey before embarking on it. This is where the Mentor comes in. Someone who has walked this path before will know what really matters, what's important along the way. The Mentor can defuse the fear of the unknown and support the hero as required, so that he can overcome his blockages and fears and actually embark on the journey. As we know, every journey starts with the first step. But before the hero can even start, he will need to prepare, and he'll need a Mentor's encouragement. That's why the Mentor archetype is essential at this stage.

What Does the Mentor Look Like?

In stories, the Mentor appears in the guise of a teacher or advisor, an experienced wise man or wise woman. This archetype guides the hero and shows him the way. Examples are Merlin the wise magician, Obi Wan Kenobi in Star Wars, Gandalf in The Lord of the Rings and Dumbledore in Harry Potter. Mentors are advisors and guides, and often have walked a similar path, so they can support the hero with their wisdom and experience. *"The hero to whom such a helper appears is typically one who has responded to the call."* (Campbell, p. 73) In everyday life it may be your grandmother, a teacher or a coach who pulls you out of the hole and helps you to rise above yourself.

The Mentor is someone who lends you support and gives you crucial advice, who encourages you to confidently embark on your journey.

Your Guru – From Darkness to Light

In India as well as other Asian countries the Mentor, who is often known as Guru or, in a Buddhist context, Lama, has a very important part to play. He or she is a teacher who has walked the spiritual path all the way to the ultimate goal. Now he can show the student how to walk his own path to enlightenment. The Guru is more than a teacher, he usually knows the student better that the student knows himself and helps him (often by unconventional ways and means) to develop whatever characteristics are required so he can reach his full potential. The term "Guru" is frequently translated as "dispeller of darkness". In Sanskrit, darkness is often taken to equal ignorance and lack of knowledge. The Sanskrit word "guru" literally means "weighty", "heavy", as in "heavy with knowledge" or "all-knowing". The hero, who is only just starting out on his journey, is "not-knowing". The Mentor's guidance, his teachings and instructions, are essential to the Hero's Journey of the spiritual hero. The relationship between a guru and his disciple, the spiritual student, is based on trust, admiration and affectionate friendship. As an all-knowing, enlightened being with supernatural powers, the Guru is equalled to God. It would be extremely difficult for the spiritual seeker to walk this path and attain the ultimate goal without the Guru's grace and help.

Your Inner Guru – the Way of the Buddha

The Future Buddha had seen the four signs during his evening walks in the park. Some scriptures say that the Devas themselves, the helpers of the Gods (in other words: angels), had come to earth to enable these moments of awareness for Siddhartha. Without these four signs – disease, old age, death, and the monk, that the charioteer had commented upon – Siddhartha would not have made the decision to walk the path of a holy man. Siddhartha learned from the Devas, his charioteer, and from his own realizations and experiences. And so he found the Inner Guru within himself.

Beware False Gurus & Mentors

On your Hero's Journey you may meet false teachers. These would-be mentors give themselves away by either expecting something from you in return for their services, or by you feeling that you cannot trust them. False gurus do not prepare you for your own Hero's Journey; instead, they try to make you dependent on them.

Your Own Hero's Journey
Homework No. 4
Meeting Your Inner Mentor

The task of the Mentor is to prepare the hero for his encounter with the unknown / the new. He is the advisor, the guide, and he equips the hero with important artefacts or character traits. However, the Guru only prepares him for the path and the unknown – the hero has to embark on his own journey and learn from his own experiences. The Mentor kind of gives him an energetic kick in the butt.

One of the tasks of the Outer Mentor is to awaken your Inner Mentor, your intuitive inner voice that will point you in the right direction. The following exercise gives you the opportunity to try and connect with your Inner Mentor.

Find a calm and relaxing place where no one will disturb you. Get comfortable, lie down or sit in a restful, meditative posture. Imagine yourself as the king or queen of your own kingdom, walking through nature. Sit on a tree trunk – grow calm and peaceful, look around. See the beautiful landscape. All this is yours. Now be ready to receive visitors and let your Mentor archetypes come to you. Prepare to be surprised at who appears and ask them what you can do to advance your journey. Ask your Inner Guru what is important for you and your kingdom, and what can be changed. Write it down...

Listen to your intuitive inner voice – it will show you the way.

Chapter 5

THE THRESHOLD TO
ANOTHER WORLD

STAGE 5.

With the fifth stage of the Hero's Journey the adventure finally begins. The hero has left all his doubts behind, is full of confidence and, at long last, embarks on his journey. The Call and his destination are much stronger within him than the Refusal. This is the moment when he cheerfully crosses the threshold to a New World. Or rather, when he *would like to* cross the threshold. Because as soon as the hero has taken the first step, he meets a Threshold Guardian, someone who will try to dissuade him from his intended journey.

The Hero's Journey – First Steps

The adventure itself begins with the crossing of the first threshold. The plane lifts off, the ship sails, this is the transition from Act 1 to Act 2. The hero has decided to embark on this journey, there is no going back now. Stage 5 is mostly about action. The hero has been in a passive state long enough, has turned things over in his mind, has had doubts, taken lessons from his Mentor, weighed things up in theory and made plans. Now, action is called for! This now is literally a matter of taking the first step into the unknown adventure, into a New World.

"Willing is not enough; we must do!" Goethe

And so, here we go! Confidently. Bags and food supplies are packed, and now the journey begins. Up to this point, the hero had to overcome much resistance, has left behind many fears and obstacles, so that now he can take off with great confidence. Having taken that first step, turning back is no longer an issue – or is it?

You Will Not Enter!

Ok, so you are leaving the Ordinary World behind. You get on the bus or the train, take your first awkward steps into the new, with confidence. But before long, up pops the first hurdle – some circumstance that makes the beginning of the journey far from easy. All beginnings are difficult! This is the first test – because at the threshold to the New World you usually find a Threshold Guardian, whose task it is to block you, send you back, unsettle you. He is there to dampen your enthusiasm, your excited energy, and have you question your journey. It may be someone from the New World such as a security guard or a customs officer of sorts who demands something from you that you don't have. It could also be someone from your Ordinary World, your mother for example, who worries about you and comes to take you back. She is crying because the journey is "too dangerous".

What will the hero do? Does he remain determined and finds a way to get past the Threshold Guardian? This first trial is essential because it is the decisive test that shows whether the hero is serious about this. The journey will be full of challenges and if he is put off by the first obstacle in his way, he will never stay the course.

The Buddha's Hero's Journey – Escape from the Golden Palace

In the case of Siddhartha, there wasn't just one Threshold Guardian but many. He and his wife Yasodhara had just had their first baby and of course she did everything she could to tie him to their new family. His son was named "Rahula", which can be translated as "impediment". King Suddhodana, Siddhartha's father, also did everything in his power to tie his heir to his role as future king. So, Siddhartha would have had all the reasons in the world to doubt and reassess his decision. But he was absolutely determined to leave his Ordinary World, meaning the office of future king, behind. And so he went to his father and told him that he planned to leave the palace. He wanted to be honest because he revered his father and explained that his destiny was to live a contemplative life in order to attain Buddha-nature, which is enlightenment. The king's reaction was to place guards on all the palace gates: Threshold

Guardians. But even though hundreds of men were guarding the palace gates, Siddhartha still managed to elude them. He began his journey at night, when they all were fast asleep – that's how he escaped to freedom.

Our Spiritual Hero's Journey

Especially during the beginning stages of our own Spiritual Hero's Journey, we tend to meet people who make us feel doubtful. Sometimes those who decide that we've suddenly gone crazy may well be our relatives or friends. A si ent retreat in a monastery? A trip to India, to an ashram? Yoga training? Cr a darshan (a meeting with a saint)? Being embraced by Amma? Critical voices in the face of such undertakings are always Threshold Guardians with only one aim: to stop your spiritual development. They themselves are happy to stay in their Ordinary World, which for many is far too comfortable to exchange for unfamiliar territory. But if you stay in your Ordinary World for too long, you may stagnate. If you ignore your heart's desires for too long, you'll end up unhappy even in your safe and prosperous home. When you are on the spiritual path, you have chosen a journey of self-actualization and self-development. Don't let anyone stop you from following this path!

Your Own Hero's Journey
Homework No. 5
Next Steps

Whenever I start something new, I use a "Next-Step-List" to carry me through the transition period from "plan" to "implementation". I simply write down whatever comes to mind that I could do first, or next.

To do this, I like to use a four-step model:

1) **Goal** - What do I want to achieve? What would be the best possible outcome?

2) **Reason** - Why? This may be the most important question as well as a strong motivator for times of resistance or hesitation. Why do I want to achieve this? Why is it important for me? Does achieving this goal make me grow? (More in Homework No. 7)

3) **Obstacles** - Why not do it? What keeps me from reaching this goal? This analysis is only helpful if you can find a possible solution to those obstacles. For example, an affirmation that you repeat every day, or a new habit, or setting an intermediary goal.

4) **Next Steps** - This fourth step is about deciding on specific actions you can take to reach your goal. It's advisable to break tasks into very small steps, so that you can tick them off one by one. You will have slow periods, just as you will have times of motivation and excitement. Step 2 helps to remind me why I want to do this in the first place…   And then: just start!

Chapter 6

ENCOUNTERING NEW FRIENDS AND ENEMIES

STAGE 6.

The hero has crossed the threshold. Now he finds himself in a New World that is exciting but also mysterious. Cautiously he steps out into this new terrain. *"Or it may be that he here discovers for the first time that there is a benign power everywhere supporting him in his superhuman passage." (Campbell, p. 97)* At this stage he encounters friends and allies as well as enemies.

New Places, New People, New Paths – A New World

The New World runs according to its own rules. The people the hero encounters are quite strange to him, so that he does not yet know whom he can trust and must approach this New World and its inhabitants with caution. His main task during this orientation phase is to become familiar with the New World and to understand and master its rules. The hero often ends up in places he's never been to before, tailor-made locations for him to get to know new people. These people are usually well-disposed towards him, but there may be intrigue, misconduct and problems with potential enemies. So, his task now is about positioning himself within this New World. This stage is also about receiving important information that will be extremely useful for the way ahead.

Travellers Must Travel

Some of your new acquaintances will attempt to hold you back. This, too, is an aspect of the New World. Your task is to develop and to clarify what it is you actually want. Stand firm and continue on your journey, and don't allow people who have no interest in their own development to stand in your way. When you are headed for a particular goal it's good to have some discipline, and part of that discipline is to not allow others to lead you astray.

This is the stage where very often the wheat is separated from the chaff. Because now more than ever you need to focus and not be swayed. Travellers must travel – and that's exactly what these trials and tribulations are about. Having set yourself free and now embarking on your very own journey, you will frighten many of those who cannot follow their heart. Each one of them will have lots of excuses when it comes to realizing their dreams. You, though, are purposefully making your own way, and there are those who will subconsciously want to stop you. Especially the Shapeshifters.

Do You Know a Shapeshifter?

As described earlier, this stage is filled with revelations. Bit by bit you'll discover who is your ally and who is your enemy. However, the Shapeshifter can be both. He appears to be your friend, someone who is very much like you. But there's one big difference. Unlike you, the Shapeshifter does not live his dreams. To the contrary – he is passive and lazy while you are full of enthusiasm and drive. You may only notice that he isn't one hundred percent well-disposed towards you once he attempts to cling to you and manipulate you so that you will let go of your goal. This, too, is a test. Do you really want to reach your goal? Then don't let anyone hold you back!

The Shapeshifter might also be someone whom you don't trust or like, but eventually you realize that you've misjudged this person. He actually does want to help you and maybe he can give you the information you need to continue your journey.

Be Yourself

Your abilities and all that you learned from your Mentor will be put to the test at this stage, including courage and sincerity. When we find ourselves in unfamiliar surroundings, we often attempt to take our cue from those around us, belittling ourselves in the process. We often don't speak our mind because we are scared to step out of line and be rejected. But if you want to find out who your true friends are and who really is on your side, you must be honest and authentic. You must be able to state your wishes and goals clearly and continue on your chosen path with your head held high. Don't be afraid to be rejected. Authenticity is your true strength. If you pretend, you will never truly know who your friends or your enemies are. The powers you gain here at this stage, as you continue on your way towards your goal, are honesty and the ability to comprehend. Be receptive. Keep learning. And be yourself.

The Buddha and the Start of His Spiritual Life

Once Siddhartha had left his palace life behind at age 29, he donned the yellow robe of an ascetic monk. He went to see famous yoga teachers and enlightened ones so he could learn from them. However, not all of them turned out to be true teachers. Although Siddhartha was keen to learn about liberation from them straight away, the Future Buddha did not instantly find his long-awaited inner peace – there is more to attaining enlightenment than a few radical spiritual practices! But even though Siddhartha's time in various monasteries did not lead to the instant liberation he was hoping for, he gained in those monasteries and ashrams the experiences that enabled him to carry on and, some time later, while on his own path, to find within himself the enlightened Buddha – his true self.

Your Own Hero's Journey
Homework No. 6
The Inner Circle

Here is an exercise I recommend to help you become aware of who is closest to you at this point in time and a good fit for you on your very own Hero's Journey:

Look at this circle.

Since you are the centre of your own universe, write your name in the centre of the circle. Now consider the people around you and ask yourself: who feels good to me right now? And whose presence makes me feel uncomfortable? Write the names of those who feel good to you into the circle close to your name, and write the other ones, the "enemies" or Shapeshifters, outside of the circle. Maybe even very far away from your inner circle. During the coming weeks, or at least for as long as possible, try to be around only those people you've placed inside the circle, because those are the people you can be yourself with and feel good about it. Just stay away from the others as best you can. There is no need to bend over backwards or pretend! Every relationship should be a sincere expression of your true self. That's why it is important to sense, to really feel certain, whom you can trust – and who is likely to think you are crazy!

Chapter 7

THE INNERMOST CAVE

STAGE 7.

Things are getting serious now. You are coming close to your goal. You have reached the point of no return. In the Hero's Journey this stage is known as "Entering the Innermost Cave" and it always involves great fear.

> *"The cave you fear to enter holds the treasure*
> *you seek."*
>
> *Joseph Campbell*

It's Getting Exciting!

The hero is making great progress on his Hero's Journey. But then, right at this stage, something happens that I refer to as: "I may be almost there but I'm dropping everything and making a run for it". It's vital not to do that and to stay with it, because this stage is the "most dangerous" so far. It wasn't easy to get to this stage, maybe it was in fact very difficult. But what is about to happen now will totally discourage you. You are so close to your goal, your dream, or an important confrontation you need to get through to reach your desired outcome, but all you want to do is drop it. It's too much, you just can't handle it. And of course, it's all very scary. Reaching your goal sometimes means that your entire life is going to radically change. And that's something most people are frightened of. Which is why this stage is predestined for self-sabotage.

Show Courage and Face Your (Inner) Enemies

This is also where you are likely to meet your Antagonist. Maybe the scales finally fall from your eyes and you begin to see who your Antagonist – your enemy – actually is. Maybe you already had a feeling about it but now you can no longer deny it, because the both of you are heading for a clash. Maybe your enemy is an inner resistance that's coming to light now. Maybe it's something that has accompanied you throughout your life, in the shape of self-doubt, lack of self-confidence, or irrational fears. It's all there, right now. This stage stands for the fight with the dragon, which is the mythological representation of our own inner resistance that keeps us from growing and reaching our goal. This, then, is where we face our fears.

No Return

To be frank, when things get unpleasant, we just want to get out of there. By this stage we often find ourselves in enemy territory, which of course makes us feel insecure. But it is vital that we overcome this fear, face whatever the unpleasant thing is, and not give in to the impulse to turn back. This is the phase of

"... the Approach to the Innermost Cave, where soon they will encounter supreme wonder and terror. It's time to make final preparations for the supreme ordeal of the adventure." (Vogler, p. 143)

The Fight for Life

This stage is sometimes referred to as "the dark night of the soul", because whatever experiences await us here, they usually feel very painful. If this is where you are right now: don't give up! You are almost home free, even though it doesn't yet feel like it. For some, this stage of their Hero's Journey feels as though a part of them is dying. I would rather regard it as a rebirth, spiritually as well as metaphorically. And a birth almost never happens without pain. People who've had a near-death experience or any other lifechanging event will know exactly what this stage is about. Everything looks bleak at first, but once you have transcended this experience, light will return to your life. Namely, from within you. Once you have mastered this crisis, you will also have obtained mastery of your life. Whatever you are learning now will so empower and shape your character that you will literally become a different person.

The Lowest Point on the Buddha's Spiritual Path

The spiritual path is about deep transformation. Saints have often obtained enlightenment by contemplation and by the experience of approaching death, because they realized that they are neither the body nor negative traits and thoughts. When you no longer identify with the false self but understand that you are the great and immortal and infinite SELF you free yourself from the outer suffering of this world and attain *moksha* (enlightenment). The Buddha had to go through hard times and asceticism in order to attain this freedom from the false self. Siddhartha lived with five Hindu ascetics and starved himself for six years to the point of emaciation and total physical exhaustion, eating nothing but one grain of rice a day. However, this harsh discipline took him no closer to his aim of enlightenment. Approaching death from starvation Siddhartha understood that this path was in opposition to the cosmic law of *ahimsa* (non-violence) and therefore could not lead to enlightenment. He left the ascetics and took up the life of an itinerant monk, and this path brought him in closer contact with the mundane world again. One day he met a beautiful woman and almost forgot about his actual goal, namely, enlightenment. This was Siddhartha's Innermost Cave that he had to transcend to finally reach his goal.

Your Own Hero's Journey

Homework No. 7

Keep Your Eye on the Goal

Homework No. 5 had us define a kind of map to reach our goal. The first step was to set the goal: "What do I want?" and the second one was to ask: "Why?"

The Innermost Cave is one of the most important stages of the Hero's Journey, and also the most dangerous because this is where many will throw in the towel. In order to victoriously emerge from this deep, dark cave or rather, to courageously face the approaching ordeal, you need one thing above all else: you need to be focused on the goal. To avoid turning back when it gets uncomfortable, you need to be fully aware of what you are fighting for and why it is important for you to reach this goal.

So, take a stack of magazines, scissors and some glue, and make a collage for your goal. At the top of the page, write what it is you wish to achieve, and then look for images that represent you having reached this goal, especially to support the emotions you'll feel when you've arrived there.

Visualize your goal and look at your collage as often as you can, especially during those times when your goal seems impossible to reach. Never forget what you are fighting for. You can do it!

SPACE FOR A SMALL VISIONBOARD COLLAGE

Chapter 8

THE ORDEAL

STAGE 8.

The day has come – the crucial fight, the make-or-break trial is here. This may be a direct confrontation or an inner process. Either way, the hero must overcome his greatest fear. This is a matter of life and death, a fight that could end in the worst possible way. Having to do battle with your Antagonist may fill you with uncertainty and tension – whether you'll win or lose is decided right here, right now. Sometimes the hero may even be in acute danger or experience a death-like moment in order to reach his goal.

Even though you may not always want to face the battle, without this essential stage you will not be able to grow. Waiting for you at the end is the Reward and the confidence that comes from having mastered a crisis.

What Is This About?

The Ordeal is a central element of the journey. Everything is at stake now. You're handing in your notice. Admitting your true feelings. Drawing a line under something. Ending a friendship. Getting married. Or divorced. Moving house. Joining an ashram, a monastery or convent. This much is certain: nothing will be as it was before.

Life is about continual transformation and change. Even though we tend to cling to circumstances, people and things, and even though we are secretly scared of big changes, it's exactly those big changes that shape and determine our lives. Once we have experienced a number of personal crises and new starts, we seem to have become a different, often more mature, version of ourselves.

So Close to Defeat

If you've ever had terrible stage fright, or faced any kind of anxiousness of such magnitude, you'll know this dreadful moment when your legs turn to jelly and your voice starts to tremble. In movies, this is the absolute dramatic climax. Sometimes, all appears to be lost, the hero believed dead, or it looks as though he may be forced to go back without reaching his goal. But that would be the wrong conclusion – nothing is as it seems!

Like a Phoenix from the Ashes

As Ada Adams said: "There is a light at the end of every tunnel." Which is a perfect description of Stage 8 of the Hero's Journey – the decisive turn-around that usually makes movie audiences rejoice. Our own journey through life is sometimes like a rollercoaster ride. And sometimes, even a dreadful accident can become a rite of passage into a new phase of life. Such moments may throw us into panic because a familiar part of ourselves falls away. But we can only master this stage if we take full responsibility for ourselves and keep control of our own life. We ourselves are the only ones who can win his crucial trial, no one else can fight this final battle on our behalf. Only by facing ourselves in this battle can we attain spiritual rebirth.

The Buddha's Final Inner Battle

In the spiritual world, the inner battle is described as a fight against demons. This is why Jesus went into the desert for 40 days and returned purified and enlightened. The Buddha decided to follow the middle path – neither radical asceticism nor luxurious secularism. And so he sat down beneath the Bodhi tree and stated his firm intention – his "sancalpa" – not to get up until he had attained enlightenment. He chose eternal inner contemplation, which he continued even after his meditation.

This stage of the Hero's Journey is not necessarily about reaching the highest level of spiritual life. There may be many other stages we need to master before we awaken and permanently realize our divine nature. Thus, from a spiritual point of view, each individual stage leads to the ultimate goal. It may be complete forgiveness and healing of inner wounds. Or the clear realization that most of us identify with a false self, followed by the intention of finding your true self. Often, this stage of the Hero's Journey is concerned with the awareness that we need to let go of something that no longer serves us, so that we can come closer to our big SELF and recognize it when we are ready. We are so much more than just the limited version of our identification that we have spent a lifetime assembling around us. We are limitless, eternal and blissful consciousness – something we simply don't have the words to adequately describe.

Your Own Hero's Journey
Homework No. 8
What Are You Most Afraid Of?

In Homework No. 3 we made a "courage list", but this exercise will go deeper. We are going to make a fear-list. Our deepest fears are often huge and paralyzing and grow even bigger when we try to suppress or sideline them. So, be brave and face the biggest of your current fears! My biggest fear was to be "alone", which is why I constantly had to be around people and found myself doing a lot of irrational things, just to avoid the possibility of feeling lonely. But the fear kept catching up with me until I found the courage to face the feeling and accept it wholeheartedly. As I accepted the fear within me, I found in my solitude: relaxation, joy, and a spiritual dimension without which my life would have remained superficial and dull.

MY LIST OF FEARS

Chapter 9

THE REWARD

STAGE 9.

Once the danger has passed and the (inner) Antagonist has finally been overcome, it's time for the Reward. It's time to celebrate life. After any massive effort, after you've reached a goal or won a fight, it's very important that you make time to claim the Reward. In fairy tales and legends this often is when the hero is handed the eagerly anticipated treasure. Or the kidnapped princess he may now take into his arms. The goal is reached, the long-awaited moment has arrived. Stage 9 presents us with the award and praise for all our troubles, all our patience, all our perseverance.

Accepting That Which We Desire

Accepting praise, recognition or any Reward may be difficult. We often work through without a break from one project to the next, one Hero's Journey to the next, and neglect to allow for the important stage of celebrating, patting ourselves on the back in whatever shape or form the Reward may take. We have courageously walked this path and have come this far, and under no circumstances must we refuse the Reward, because the result of our effort is of great value and must be marked out as such, otherwise it would be as though we hadn't even been on a Hero's Journey. That's what this stage is about. You have fought and striven for this, and finally you have achieved it. Now you have every right to celebrate your achievements and accept what is your due. This is extremely important, because without Stage 9, the stage of assessment, the Hero's Journey will be without completion.

Your Own Hero's Journey

Homework No. 9

Life is a celebration – celebrate!

This is where you leave all humbleness and modesty behind and just celebrate! Celebrate life and celebrate your own achievements. That's the best and most appropriate way to bid good-bye to this phase of your life. You may feel a little down in the dumps because the journey may have been so intense and draining, but it's important to make time for the celebration of all you have achieved. Even if it's just a very small gesture, such as opening a bottle of bubbly or treating yourself to something nice. In the movies, there is usually the big wedding, the victory celebration or the farewell party. The great adventure is coming to an end and now it's your turn. How can you treat and reward yourself for your Hero's Journey? And even if it hasn't quite finished yet – we can all use a little motivational nudge!

LIST IDEAS FOR CELEBRATING LIFE:

Chapter 10

THE ROAD BACK

STUFE 10.

The worst appears to be over. The hero is already on the way back. This is the stage where the hero decides that he will in fact return to the Ordinary World. But somehow, he just can't shake the feeling that there's something more to come. In the movies, this is the beginning of the third act, when things very often turn out to be not as they appear. This is so that the hero can undergo one final ordeal which often is a result of the ordeal he has just gone through. It's a final test to ascertain whether the hero has really grown (up), whether he has really learned from his exploits.

The Adventure Has Not Yet Ended

After the big celebration, the hero turns his back on the by now familiar New World, intending to go back to his Ordinary World. But he notices very quickly that something isn't quite right yet. Sometimes you overcome a problem only to find yourself facing another challenge that's directly connected to having solved the original problem. It's like when you tidy up. It won't do to just superficially gloss over things – sometimes you can't even see the full extent of the chaos you need to sort out until you have completed the initial tidying up. In the movies, this is when the hero is again attacked by dark forces intent on taking their revenge.

The road back will show us that we have not yet completed the task at hand, and that a further, final ordeal awaits, often within ourselves.

What You Really Need

Sometimes it isn't until the hero is on the way back that he realizes something essential is still missing, even though he did reach his goal. In film terminology we call this the difference between "want" (the conscious wish for something), meaning, the obvious objective of the story, and "need" (the subconscious inner desire). The "want" is a specific goal: a medal or some other award, a new job, a promotion, a treasure, or a new relationship. But the "need" is what the protagonist really desires, what he still craves deep inside. It may be hard to define and often it has no shape or form. For example, it may be self-confidence, inner peace, love, approval or contentment. Stage 10 of the Hero's Journey reveals this inner need and the hero comes to realize what his TRUE goal is. Now, it's about the inner journey which, from this stage onwards, is also part of the outer Hero's Journey.

The Buddha and Life After Enlightenment

There is still a life to be lived after achieving the ultimate goal, even after enlightenment. As a Zen monk so aptly put it:

"After enlightenment, the laundry."

When the Buddha had reached his TRUE goal, he realized that his own personal self-actualization was not enough, and he understood that he would need to help others complete their own journey.

Your Own Hero's Journey

Homework No. 10

The Search for Your Deepest Desire

We all have lots of aims and wishes in our life, many of which we achieve or fulfil. A wish will often give away your deepest desire, the one that is difficult to put into words. The wish for a new job might be the expression of a deep longing for security or a more fulfilled life. The wish for a relationship could be about the need for self-love and acceptance. And wanting to travel might be about a longing for freedom and spontaneity. Behind most of our aims and wishes are hidden messages from our soul. And sometimes, when we have reached what we set out for, we notice that this is not yet it – something is still missing. Our innermost desires are often hard to understand. It takes a lot of courage to dare to look at what's behind our outer wishes. But that's exactly what we are going to do.

Make a list of your current goals and wishes (left-hand column) and next to it, in the right-hand column, write your corresponding deepest desires behind them. (For example: want: A house on the countryside, need: peace of mind)

WANT   NEED

WANT   NEED

This is just for you – you needn't show this to anyone. Any insights revealed are for your eyes only.

Chapter 11

TRANSFORMATION

STAGE 11.

The last-but-one phase is the most crucial, because it's where our hero, like a butterfly after its metamorphosis, learns what it is to fly. This is the resurrection, the final (inner) ordeal, one more crisis our hero must surrender to. The hero will be purged by this experience and reborn as someone new. For one last time, he surrenders to his fears and anxieties and faces up to that which he needs to do. Only once he takes the leap of faith to complete this final step can he then return home with his head held high – a true hero.

> *"Resurrection is the hero's final exam, her chance to show what she has learned. Heroes are totally purged by final sacrifice or deeper experience of the mysteries of life and death. Some don't make it past this dangerous point, but those who survive go on to close the circle of the Hero's Journey when they Return with the Elixir." (Vogler, p. 212)*

One final move on the chessboard of life, one final battle, is required before the hero can return home. This may be an inner dispute or an outer one.

You Return Home a Different Person

Stage 11 is called Transformation or Resurrection – an inner resurrection. Maybe because, by now, we are certain that, as we are a part of the greater whole, we benefit from the guidance and protection that the divine greater whole affords us. At this stage, intuition is more important than ever. By now we know exactly what is right and good for us. Our soul's desires are no longer just by-products of our original goal but, having achieved this goal, we now finally understand what is important to us in our life. Constantly stepping outside of our comfort zone shapes our character, and those changes are necessary for growth, maturity and our inner strength.

A Matter of Letting Go Completely and of Forgiveness

This stage offers a crucial transformation. The hero now acts in keeping with his outer goal as well as his inner needs. This is also the stage where we clear up all conflicts. Instead of holding on to resentment and old wounds, we have accepted, forgiven and released it all. Now we can return home.

Surrendering and Becoming a Conduit for Inner Wisdom

As previously mentioned, Stage 11 is about the discovery of a spiritual journey, our inner compass that tells us our life has purpose, and that our talents were given to us for a reason. Eastern philosophy uses the term "dharma", not to be confused with "karma" which means "cause and effect of our actions". Dharma is often translated as "the path of righteousness", but it also means living in harmony with our own true nature. When we express our inner being, we fulfil our soul's desire. That's something we are very much aware of internally. When you, for example, feel comfortable doing your work because it's in harmony with your own talents, your work will flow easily and joyfully. That's what dharma is: following your intuition, doing what feels right. Following the imprint of your given talents and, by your actions, contributing and giving back to the world something of your true self. Stage 11 asks that you trust in a higher guidance and place yourself at its disposal, becoming an instrument in the hands of a divine power.

Your Own Hero's Journey

Homework No. 11

Connecting with Eternity

I have no doubt that there is something deep within "what holds the world together at the core". (Goethe, Faust). You can't see it, of course, but when you begin to search for God, you will most certainly find Her or Him. Proof positive is synchronicity: we focus on a particular subject matter and at every turn we seem to come across it. Some would call it coincidence, or that we are more receptive to things once they become important to us. But I believe this is living proof of how the universe works, and a direct response from "up high". If you won't or can't believe this, I invite you to try the following:

Within your innermost Self, ask a question that's important to you and that ro one except for a higher power can provide an answer to. Pay attention during the following days and listen out for the answer, which may reach you in any number of ways. Newspapers, cinema, accidentally overheard conversations on the train – in my experience, your question or rather, the answer to your question, will return to you like a boomerang. You are never alone.

NOTES OF ANSWERS AND SYNCHRONICITY

Chapter 12

BACK HOME

STAGE 12.

The hero has done what he set out to do – this Hero's Journey is coming to an end. The hero returns home to the Ordinary World, back to where his folks are anxiously waiting for him. It is very likely that he has reached his goal, but most importantly, he has found a precious treasure within himself. His newly acquired knowledge, insights and experiences have changed him. Now he can see inner qualities such as love, freedom, wisdom and patience from another, more mature perspective. Sometimes his greatest gain is his own story that he can now relay to his beloved people back home. The hero becomes a Mentor.

Like Christmas and Birthday Rolled into One

It will all be alright in the end, and if it's not alright then it's not yet the end. Sometimes, in a comedy, the foolish hero hasn't learned from his mistakes and experiences at all, and immediately goes back to the same silly habits as before. And that will be the start of a new Hero's Journey… All the festivities are over, all the tales have been told. Now what?

The Great Potential of Emptiness

The epic journey is over, it's the day after the great opening, the book has been published. The goal has been reached. Now what? A yawning void?

Our society fears boredom, emptiness and leisure – we are anxious when we don't use our time "productively". But if we go back in time and remember our childhood, were we ever bored for any length of time? Doesn't the empty space encourage wonderful new ideas and lead to more Hero's Journeys? Our world is amazing, there is always so much to discover!

The Hero May Need to Embark on Another Journey

Some time has passed, and we've settled back into everyday life. But although things should be perfectly fine now, we feel that they aren't. There is yet another Call within us, maybe about a new issue or parts of the old one, but something urges us towards another journey. Life renews itself in every moment. A new summit to be climbed, a new award to be won, a new goal to be reached – we cannot avoid it. After the Hero's Journey is before the Hero's Journey...

The Hero Becomes a Hermit and Embarks on an Inner Journey

It's not as though every hero returning home with all the experiences gained on his Hero's Journey will feel like a total stranger. But often, being back home is quite difficult. Sometimes we question our entire existence – but maybe all we really need is some time to digest our experiences. It is perfectly right and important to allow the required space for processing each experience. Which sometimes is only possible by temporarily withdrawing from society. But not to worry, no hermit is ever forced to be alone. Rather, it's his deepest wish for calmness and growth, for inner peace and meditation or a life in harmony with nature, that makes him seek out solitude. Thus, after completing the outer journey, the inner journey sometimes becomes a new Hero's Journey.

The Hero Stays at Home

Hero is hero. It doesn't matter whether he embarks on a new journey or decides to stay at home. Often, the greatest challenge can be to achieve happiness within the ordinary-life environment. The hero might also eventually become a Mentor for those who are embarking on similar journeys. Your experiences will allow you to pass on valuable information to someone just setting out to pursue their goal, much like you did at one time!

Your Own Hero's Journey

Homework No. 12

Enjoy your life!

Homework No. 12 asks you to actively pursue your own wellbeing. Being happy can be so easy! A delicious cup of tea, a good book, time with friends or family or out in the countryside. And nothing for you to do but relax and assimilate your experiences. All those impressions you've gathered during your travels are like the icing on a cake: they will need time to set. It often takes a long time to understand what you have achieved, and it's important to celebrate those achievements! Right now, there's nothing to be done but enjoy your life and, if required, share whatever lessons you've learned during your Hero's Journey. Rest in your inner calmness and grow strong again – in anticipation of your next Hero's Journey!

All's well that ends well!

SUMMERY

I'd like to end my little exploration of the Hero's Journey with a brief summary. During the writing process you experience quite a few ups and downs, but you can always stop and smell the roses. I hope this outline of a Hero's Journey will contribute as much to your life as it did to mine, when I first came across it all those years ago!

I believe that, during our lifetime, we embark on numerous Hero's Journeys, and even though we don't complete every single one, we always learn something about ourselves and the deepest desires of our soul. For me, it's incredibly enriching to view my life as a fairy tale, or rather, a *Hero's Journey*. It gives me the courage to imagine that I can achieve all my deepest wishes and longings – and then go for it! During our Hero's Journeys we go down into the deepest recesses of our soul, do battle with inner foes such as self-doubt, and sometimes with more mundane monsters, Threshold Guardians who make it hard for us to proceed. But if we look at life as a game and enjoy it like a child, we can certainly reach all our goals and eventually return home, victorious and transformed.

Our greater home, the eternal SELF.

I wish you a good Hero's Journey, at whichever stage of it you may be right now.

And just in case you've lost your way, here is the schedule again, and a brief summation. Think about your personal heroes Journey, and add it below.

12 STEPS OF THE HERO'S JOURNEY

ACT 1:
THE DECISION TO EMBARK ON A THE SPIRITUAL PATH

When did you start your spiritual path, the search for purpose, God or enlightenment… ?

STAGE 1 — THE BEGINNING: THE ORDINARY WORLD

The journey begins in the cosy Ordinary World, the comfort zone where all is well but there's no development, no growth (yet).

How did your Comfort Zone look like?

STAGE 2 - THE CALL TO ADVENTURE

An awareness of something missing, or the sudden appearance
of a new task that forces the hero to leave his Ordinary World.

The first inciting incident on your spiritual way?

STAGE 3 — THE REFUSAL

The hero is scared, hesitant, and doesn't know whether to follow the Call, which is
getting increasingly louder. He is afraid to give up his security and reluctant to step
into the unknown.

Did you had any fears on the way? Write down your refusals.

STAGE 4 — MEETING WITH THE MENTOR / GURU

Meeting a Guru or Mentor finally convinces the hero to embark on the journey.
He gathers information and learns about matters that will be of use during the
journey. Encouraged, he sets off.

Think about your teachers on this way. Who helped you the most?
Do have a Guru or even more than one?

ACT 2:

JOURNEY INTO THE UNKNOWN

STAGE 5 — THE DEPARTURE

The hero has gathered all his courage, has overcome his initial reluctance and
now, finally, the journey can begin. But before he has even really started,
he has to get past the Threshold Guardian.

What or who was your Threshold Guardian?

STAGE 6 — ENCOUNTERING NEW FRIENDS AND ENEMIES

Having taken the first hurdle, the hero now faces the next lot of challenges.
The focus of this stage is on new friends and allies, but also new enemies.
new ordeals and new accomplishments. The hero continues the journey but
reaching his goal might be harder than expected!

*If you start your way, your realize there is Grace and something called
beginners luck. What was easy from the beginning on?
And what was hard for you on the spiritual path?*

STAGE 7 — THE CAVE / DARK NIGHT OF THE SOUL

Some time into the journey, the hero finds himself in a dangerous place: The
Innermost Cave. This is where he will soon face an outer battle, but also, more
importantly, the inner battle (against his own inner resistances and projections).

Your inner battles:

STAGE 8 — THE FIGHT FOR THE ELIXIR

The stage of the confrontation. This is where the battle takes place, or the conflict, or whatever deed needs to be done. The Reward is the hero's transformation. Sometimes the hero receives the actual desired Elixir or the treasure, and sometimes he doesn't. But the treasure could also be an inner knowledge gained through the experience of the Hero's Journey.

Write down the main conflict/confrontations.
Which whom, why and when did you fight?

ACT 3:

RETURNING WITH WHAT WE'VE GAINED

STAGE 9 — THE SECOND THRESHOLD

The hero crosses the threshold back into the Ordinary World where he started out from. But something causes him to hesitate.
Has he really achieved everything he set out for?

How did you find the solution / win the fight?

STAGE 10 — THE ROAD BACK

Returning home is more difficult than expected. The hero encounters new enemies or has to overcome disbelief and deal with incomprehension. In order to make it through this final ordeal he has to integrate into his actions everything he has learned and obtained during his Hero's Journey.

Think about your friends, family and relatives – did you lost support or friendships on the way, because of "You have changed?"

STAGE 11 — TRANSFORMATION / RENEWAL

Finally, our hero has become a master of both worlds. His inner development increases. He integrates his new-found knowledge into his everyday life and shares his discoveries with his surroundings.

Did you experience something higher?
How did you transform and grow spiritually on your way?

STAGE 12 — BACK HOME (WITH THE ELIXIR)

Having returned home, the hero shares his adventures with his people and becomes a Mentor for quite a few others who wish to grow or embark on a journey…

Can you become a Mentor yourself? And help others on their way?

MY HEROE'S JOURNEY MANIFESTO

#1 You are free!

#2 You were given certain talents in this life –
it's up to you to use them well!

#3 Your life is your own personal Hero's Journey –
you alone write the script and direct the play!

#4 If you don't yet know what you want, keep
searching until you find it

#5 It is your (and everybody else's) birth-right to
grow and to be happy!

#6 When you've found what you really want to do,
do it! Don't be deterred, not by others and not by
yourself!

#7 After every new beginning, every decision and
every courageous first step, a new world awaits!

#8 Hesitation is natural, but don't unnecessarily delay the most important decision of your life! Making no decision is often much worse than failing.

#9 Your path may lead through dark caves, you may encounter monsters, be they internal or external. Just remember: you are stronger than they are! Don't let anyone or anything tell you that you can't do it – especially not your inner critic!

#10 Even if you fall – it's much better than never even trying!

#11 Learn from your mistakes and trust that all wounds will heal. Take your time. Then let them go. Remember: you can always get up again and carry on walking!

#12 It's not about the destination, it's about the journey. Not about a result but about the process.

#13 A hero lives in the "now". Forget about planning for the future and living in the past and enjoy what you really have, right here and NOW!

#14 When you don't know what to do, go out into nature – Mother Nature has so much wisdom for you!

#15 Try to take one step at a time and, in spite of the massive sensory overload all around, learn to FOCUS!

#16 True kindness opens all the locked doors!

#17 Be brave, humble and gentle at the same time! Balance is achieved by a mixture of feminine and male energies.

#18 Don't set out to hurt anyone, not even yourself. Never! Neither in thought, word or deed. If you do, you'll live to regret it.

#19 Help others and help yourself. Learn to accept help!

#20 Be easy about it. Allow some time each day for relaxation. Find ways to recharge your batteries and learn to look after your energy!

#21 Be inspired! Find ways to enjoy your life. Notice the little things that make you happy and brighten your day!

#22 Try to have only those around you who are good for you and avoid those who aren't! Be motivated, but never allow anyone to drag you down and discourage you. Don't allow anyone to block you, and ensure that your innermost energy field remains clear, so it may vibrate without obstruction.

#23 Take NOTHING personally and don't allow grievances to fester over a long period of time.

#24 If nothing else works, say to yourself: "This, too, will pass."

#25 The universe is enormous, and possibilities appear to be endless. If you feel lost and can't see a way forward, take some time for yourself in solitude. You have all the answers within you and your intuition will show you the way.

#26 Try to be like you were when you were a child: open, happy, in the here and now, creative and a wild enjoyer of life!

#27 Use exclamation marks!!! Live with exclamation marks!!!

Straight from the heart!!! And filled with zest for life!!!

Do whatever makes you happy!!! And enjoy your journey of life !!!

.

LIFE HAS NO MEANING. EACH OF US HAS MEANING AND WE BRING IT TO LIFE.

- J. CAMPBELL

NOTES